THE
FOUR FREEDOMS

Freedom to Worship

by Bryon Cahill

RED
CHAIR
·PRESS·

Please visit our website at **www.redchairpress.com**.
Find a free catalog of all our high-quality products for young readers.

 For a free activity page for this book, go to
www.redchairpress.com and look for Free Activities.

Freedom to Worship

Publisher's Cataloging-In-Publication Data
(Prepared by The Donohue Group, Inc.)

Cahill, Bryon.
Freedom to worship / by Bryon Cahill.
p. : ill. (some col.) ; cm. -- (The four freedoms)
Summary: The freedom to worship is a sacred right protected by the First Amendment
to the U.S. Constitution. Learn how the freedom to express one's religious beliefs
continues to be a major source of conflict around the world.
Interest age level: 009-012.
ISBN: 978-1-937529-92-5 (lib. binding/hardcover)
ISBN: 978-1-937529-84-0 (pbk.)
ISBN: 978-1-937529-97-0 (eBook)
1. Freedom of religion--Juvenile literature. 2. Freedom of religion. I. Title.
KF4783 .C34 2013

342.73/0852   2012951568

Edited by: Jessica Cohn
Designed by: Dinardo Design
Photo credits: Cover, title page, table of contents, p. 15, 21, 23, 27, 29: Dreamstime; p. 5: FDR Library; p. 6,
7, 10, 12: Shutterstock; p. 9: AP Photo; p. 13, 16, 18: Bettmann/Corbis/APPhoto; p. 14: Getty Images; p. 17:
UN Photo; p. 19: Franka Bruns/AP Photo; p. 20: Nassar Nassar/AP Photo; p. 22: JD Pooley/AP Photo; p. 25:
Winfried Rothermel/AP Photo; p. 26: Ng Han Guan/AP Photo

This series first published by:

Red Chair Press LLC   PO Box 333   South Egremont, MA 01258-0333

Printed in the United States of America

1 2 3 4 5 18 17 16 15 14

Table of Contents

Freedom for Faiths

"We are a nation of many nationalities, many races, many religions bound together by a single unity, the unity of freedom and equality. … Whoever seeks to set one religion against another, seeks to destroy all religion."

— *Franklin Delano Roosevel*

The year was 1940. Franklin Delano Roosevelt, also known as FDR, was president of the United States. He had been president for two terms. He was running for third time when he spoke these words at a November 1 campaign rally in Brooklyn, New York.

Europe was in the middle of World War II. Germany and Italy had invaded Denmark, Norway, France, Egypt, Greece and other nations. There were reports of Jews being held as prisoners in Germany. In the speech FDR asked people to stay strong and help one another. He reminded them that the U.S. was a nation that respected all people and religions.

Franklin Delano Roosevelt, or FDR, was president from 1933 to 1945. He served three full terms and part of a fourth.

World's Largest Religions

The world is a big place. There are more than seven billion people. Around the world, there are more than 20 major religions. Each has different branches.

Christianity is the world's largest religion. It has more than two billion followers. The people in this faith believe in one God and Jesus. Christians believe Jesus is the son of God and follow his teachings.

The second largest religion is Islam. People who practice this faith are called Muslims. About a quarter of the people in the world are Muslims. They believe in God. Muslims follow the teachings of Muhammad, the founder of Islam.

Did You Know?

The five major groups of Christianity are Roman Catholic, Eastern Orthodox, Oriental Orthodox, Anglican, and Protestant branches. Each has different beliefs. Many Christians, however, belong to smaller branches or denominations within these major religions.

Other Faiths

Together, the two largest faiths have more than four billion people. That is more than half of the **population** in the world. About two billion people follow other faiths. Another billion people say they have no religion.

Many people with no religion still think there is a higher power. They just do not believe in one set of ideas. Even people in the same faith do not always think the same way.

For this reason and others, people in the U.S. are allowed to choose how to worship. In 1940, FDR brought attention to this fact. The world was at war, and people were fighting for this kind of freedom.

Did You Know?

There are three major branches of Islam: Sunni, Shi'a, and Sufism. Each branch has different beliefs. Some Muslims are part of smaller branches.

CHAPTER 1

Freedom of Worship

"Freedom prospers when religion is vibrant and the rule of law under God is acknowledged."

—Ronald Reagan

Like President Ronald Reagan in the 1980s, FDR often spoke of freedom and God. He knew his messages would reach the entire world. Each January, FDR gave a speech to **Congress**. Presidents still do today in a speech called the State of the Union.

On January 6, 1941, FDR made a speech now known as the Four Freedoms speech. He talked about four basic rights for all people.

- Freedom of speech and expression
- Freedom to worship
- Freedom from want
- Freedom from fear

It was the height of World War II. Many free nations were falling to their enemies. With his words, FDR was sending a message of hope to people around the world.

When FDR was campaigning for a third term, France and other free nations in Europe had already been taken over by the Nazi government of Germany.

Protection by Law

The freedoms FDR talked about are part of U.S. law. The right to worship is found in the U.S. Constitution. That is the agreement that lays out the first laws of the land.

Congress makes laws in the U.S. Capitol. The 1st U.S. Congress met in 1789.

The Bill of Rights is part of that agreement. It offers ten important amendments, or changes, to the Constitution. These changes were added in 1791, four years after the Constitution was approved.

The First Amendment talks about the freedom of worship. It says, "Congress shall make no law respecting an establishment of religion, or **prohibiting** the free exercise thereof."

This means the government is not in charge of religion. Instead, people are allowed to have their own beliefs. This right is part of the American way.

Roots of Belief

Throughout U.S. history, the nation's leaders have been freedom fighters. The United States was formed in 1776. The early Americans fought a war with Great Britain in order to be free of English rule.

Long before then, the land was home to Native Americans. Then sailors from Spain arrived. In the 1500s, people from Spain explored this New World. They traveled into what is now the United States.

The Spanish were looking for spices, furs, and gold. They took over the land and riches they found. They had horses and guns, and the Native Americans did not.

Did You Know?

In 1492, an explorer named Christopher Columbus landed on an island in the Caribbean. People often say that Columbus discovered America, but this is not exactly true. A Viking named Leif Erikson had arrived in North America about 350 years earlier.

Clash of Faiths

In the 1500s, Spain had Catholic rulers. Everyone in Spain had to follow the faith of the kings and queens. The explorers from Spain brought their religion with them.

The native peoples of North and South America had their own beliefs. Some listened to what the settlers had to say. Others fought the Spanish and their ideas.

Many of the Spanish settlers came to believe it was God's plan to **convert** the natives to the Catholic faith. In the history of the world, many battles have been fought over religion. In America, these differences were in place from the start.

Some of the first Spanish settlers built missions for the Roman Catholic faith.

Puritans in America

Soon after, other people followed the Spanish from Europe to America. Many people came looking for furs and gold. Others came in search of religious freedom.

The region the English Puritans settled is still called New England today.

In the 1600s, most people in England worshipped in the Church of England. The king ran the church. A group called the Puritans wanted to break from the king's church. They did not agree with the views of the state religion. The Puritans wanted to worship freely.

This was not easy to do. Charles the First was the king. He punished people who spoke out with new ideas. The Puritans were **persecuted**.

In the 1600s, a group of Puritans sailed for freedom. They landed on the northeast coast of America and called their new home Plymouth. There, they began their new lives.

House of Prayer

Over the years, people from all over the world came to America. About 150 years after the Puritans arrived, the new nation's founders wanted to unite people. And they did not want to have a king or leader force one belief on all people again. So they made laws that allowed for religious freedom.

America today is known as the land of the free. People are free to believe in the God they choose. They can worship alone in their own homes. Or they can choose to take part in services with others.

Christians can gather in churches. Muslims can pray together in **mosques**. Buddhists can go to monasteries or temples. People of the Jewish faith can worship at **synagogues**. In these houses of prayer, people can meet without fear of being punished.

Various U.S. laws protect houses of prayer and worship.

Protecting Religious Freedom

By law, people in America can worship the way they want. Yet there are people who do not respect religions other than their own. Some people bully those of different faiths. Being free to worship does not mean being free of hate.

The U.S. government promises this freedom and protects this right. The law does not tell people what to believe. But it does tell them how they can act. A person who harms someone because of his or her religion can be arrested. Hurting others for their faith or belief is called a hate crime.

When Fear Becomes Real

The people who carried out attacks on America on September 11, 2001, were Islamic extremists. This means that they believe in something that most Muslims find extreme and wrong. Some Americans did not understand this at first. After the attacks, many Muslims in America were afraid. They had to deal with people who feared and hated them. Officials had to explain that there is a difference between being Muslim and being a terrorist.

Nearly 3,000 people were killed by terrorists in the 9/11 attacks, including many American Muslims.

CHAPTER 2

Free to Worship: Yesterday and Today

"Everyone has the right to freedom of religion. This includes freedom to change one's religion or belief, and to express his religion in teaching and worship."

— *The Universal Declaration of Human Rights*

After World War II ended, many nations began to stand behind FDR's ideas. In 1945, the United Nations (U.N.) formed. In 1948, the U.N. created a list of rights that every person should have. This was called the Universal Declaration of Human Rights.

One person who helped write the list was Eleanor Roosevelt. She was FDR's wife. The first lady was a member of the U.N. Human Rights Commission. She believed in freedoms for all, just as FDR did.

The United Nations (U.N.) is an important group of world leaders. There are 193 countries that take part in the U.N. The leaders discuss the world's problems and look for peaceful solutions.

The Holocaust

World War II helped the world understand the need to protect people's freedoms. During the war, Jews and others were persecuted in Europe. Many people chose to **boycott** Jewish-owned businesses. The Jewish people lost their freedom to worship. Millions of them also lost their lives.

The leader of Germany blamed many troubles on the Jews. He taught others to believe that they were less than human. He spread hatred throughout his army and country. This part of history is known as the **Holocaust**.

German soldiers hold signs reading "Germans defend yourself! Don't buy from Jews!"

A Symbol of Faith

The Germans destroyed Jewish homes and businesses during World War II. They rounded up Jews and forced them to wear the Star of David, a symbol of the Jewish faith. They even wrote the German word for "Jew" on the stars.

German soldiers looked for the badge to separate Jews from other kinds of people. The Jews were forced to work in labor camps. There, they were beaten, starved, and killed.

Millions of Jews were murdered because of their faith. At the start of the war, it was difficult for Americans to believe millions could be murdered because of their religion. Today, the U.N. and others work hard to keep this type of tragedy from happening again.

Did You Know?

The word *Holocaust* means "great destruction of life." Six million Jews were murdered because of their religion during the Holocaust. That was about two-thirds of Europe's Jewish population.

Religious Freedom Denied

Many nations have signed the U.N. agreement. The right to worship is not **universal**, however. In Egypt, people carry national identification cards. Until 2012, the cards listed each

Egyptians must carry identification cards.

person's religion. Only three faiths were allowed. A person could be Muslim, Christian, or Jewish. People who practiced a religion called Bahá'í were persecuted.

In Iran, people of the Bahá'í faith have been turned away from hospitals. They have been kept out of schools. Their homes have been burned. Some have even been killed.

Did You Know?

The Bahá'í faith is based on belief in one God with many messengers across time. Many Christians and Muslims do not agree with the Bahá'í belief that other messengers, or prophets, from God followed Jesus and Muhammad.

Christian Persecution

Many Christians are persecuted today. The largest numbers of people who are harmed because of what they believe in are Christian. Much of the hate directed at them happens in the Middle East.

In Saudi Arabia, a person cannot own items for any faith other than Islam. If people are caught with a **crucifix** or Star of David, they can be arrested. A Muslim who becomes Christian risks death in many Islam lands. This is one reason why many people flee their homelands. Those who leave their countries in fear are called refugees.

The ancient city of Jerusalem is a holy city with many sacred sites for Christians, Muslims, and Jews.

Right to Change

It is not always people of different faiths who fight. Some larger groups of Muslims persecute smaller groups of Muslims. Some branches of Christians fight with other Christians.

The U.N. declaration talks about the right to worship, but it does not guarantee the right. In every part of the world, people are still persecuted for who they are and what they believe in. The fight for religious freedom continues.

At the heart of the matter is the right of people to think for themselves. Freedom means having and making choices. It means that people can worship as they choose. Or they can decide to not be religious at all. People can be raised one way and change.

Buddhism is one of the fastest-growing faith groups in the U.S.

Source: National Endowment for the Humanities

Protestant by Law

The people of the United Kingdom can worship as they chose. At least, most of them can. But not everyone has this right.

How can this be? The laws do not force religion on the citizens of England or Wales, for example. And there are many Catholics and Muslims in the United Kingdom. Yet the royal family is not allowed to choose; they must be Christian.

The British monarch is the head of the Church of England.

The Church of England is a branch of the Protestant faith. It is the state religion, and the king or queen is supposed to lead it. In effect, a person cannot become the king or queen unless he or she is a Protestant.

Did You Know?

The word *Protestant* comes from a Latin word meaning "one who publicly declares or protests." In 1517, a Catholic named Martin Luther nailed a list to a church door in Germany. It listed the things he thought were wrong with the Catholic Church. This protest led to the beginning of the Protestant branch of Christianity.

Promoting Religious Freedom

"This is my simple religion. There is no need for temples; no need for complicated philosophy. Our own brain, our own heart is our temple; the philosophy is kindness."

—*Dalai Lama*

The Dalai Lama is the spiritual leader of Tibetan Buddhism, which is based in an area of Asia. He often travels around the world.

The Dalai Lama is a peaceful man. He believes that all people should be kind to one another. This leader believes in the freedom of worship for all. He does not believe that people need to pray in churches and temples.

Millions of people enjoy hearing him speak in public. He is not allowed in his own land, however. China is in charge of Tibet now, and China does not allow him to be there.

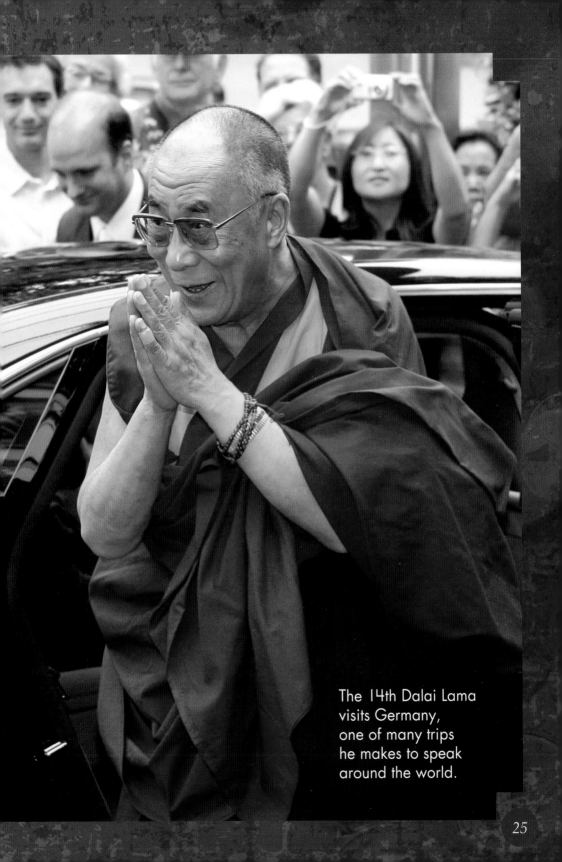

The 14th Dalai Lama
visits Germany,
one of many trips
he makes to speak
around the world.

Working to Make It Better

Many wars have been fought over religion. But people do not have to fight to change things. There are peaceful ways to solve problems.

There are still many people around the world who practice their religions in fear. Many groups of people think this is wrong and are working to change this. One of them is the United States Commission on International Religious Freedom.

This group keeps watch on places where people are persecuted for their beliefs. The group makes reports about these countries. It gives recommendations to the U.S. government.

China closely watches the religious and political activities of the Uighers, a Muslim group.

The Right to Choose

It is important that groups like the United States Commission on International Religious Freedom continue their work. FDR believed each person should be able to worship in his or her own way. A government should not decide this for anyone.

This is what FDR meant when he gave his famous Four Freedoms speech. Choosing a faith or choosing no religion at all should be up to each person.

The best way to celebrate freedoms is to use them.

In free countries, people worship without fear in churches, mosques, and synagogues. People who are not free must worship in secret and in fear.

If you pray, you can be thankful for the freedom to do so. You can ask that those who do not yet have this right be given the freedom you have. And if you chose not to worship, be thankful you have that choice to make.

Glossary

boycott — refuse to buy or handle goods as a form of protest

Congress — law-making body of the U.S. government made up of the Senate and the House of Representatives

convert — to cause a change in one's belief

crucifix — representation of a cross, often with a figure of Jesus on it

Holocaust — mass killing of Jews and others carried out by the Nazis during WWII

mosques — places where Muslims worship and pray

persecuted — made to suffer for a belief or for something that cannot be changed

population — total number of people in a city, state, country, or other area

prohibiting — to forbid by law or by another authority

synagogues — Jewish houses of worship and prayer

universal — of or affecting the whole world or all people

In FDR's Words

In the future days, which we seek to make secure, we look forward to a world founded upon four essential human freedoms. The first is freedom of speech and expression—everywhere in the world. The second is freedom of every person to worship God in his own way—everywhere in the world. The third is freedom from want—which, translated into world terms, means economic understandings which will secure to every nation a healthy peacetime life for its inhabitants—everywhere in the world. The fourth is freedom from fear—which, translated into world terms, means a world-wide reduction of armaments to such a point and in such a thorough fashion that no nation will be in a position to commit an act of physical aggression against any neighbor—anywhere in the world. That is no vision of a distant millennium. It is a definite basis for a kind of world attainable in our own time and generation. That kind of world is the very antithesis of the so-called new order of tyranny which the dictators seek to create with the crash of a bomb.

—from FDR's address to Congress, January 6, 1941

Additional Resources

BOOKS

Clark, Beth. *Anne Hutchinson (Colonial Leaders)*. New York, NY: Chelsea House Publications, 2000.

Elmer, Robert. *Promise of Zion* series. Ada, MI: Bethany House Publishers, 2000.

Evans, Freddi Williams. *Hush Harbor: Praying in Secret*. Minneapolis, MN: Carolrhoda Books; Lerner Publishing Group, 2008.

Krull, Kathleen. *A Kid's Guide to America's Bill of Rights: Curfews, Censorship, and the 10-Pound Giant*. New York, NY: HarperCollins, 1999.

Kudlinski, Kathleen. *Franklin Delano Roosevelt: Champion of Freedom*. New York, NY: Aladdin Publishers; Simon and Schuster, 2003.

Turner, Juliette. *Our Constitution Rocks*. Grand Rapids, MI: Zonderkidz; Zondervan Publishing, 2012.

WEB SITES

First Amendment Schools: *Educating for freedom and responsibility*
http://www.firstamendmentschools.org

The Illinois First Amendment Center: *Promoting rights through education*
http://www.illinoisfirstamendmentcenter.com/religion.php

WEB SITES (*cont*)

United States Commission on International Religious Freedom
http://www.uscirf.gov

United States Holocaust Memorial Museum: *Introduction to the Holocaust*
http://www.ushmm.org/wlc/en/article.php?ModuleId=10005143

INTERACTIVE RESOURCES

fdr4freedoms Digital Resource: *Videos, biographies, and interactive timeline*
http://fdr4freedoms.org

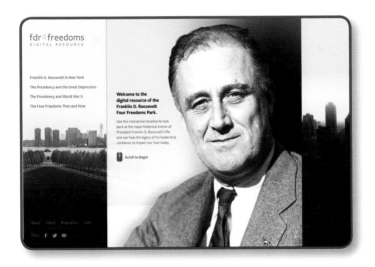

Index

Bryon Cahill has been writing for young people for over a decade. As editor of Weekly Reader's *READ* magazine, Bryon wrote short fiction, nonfiction, and reader's theater plays; created award-winning literary websites; and spearheaded an experimental theater adaptation of William Shakespeare's *Much Ado About Nothing* live on Facebook. An avid reader, Bryon also enjoys running and playing tennis at home in Morristown, New Jersey.